DK Eye Wonder

Rocks and Minerals

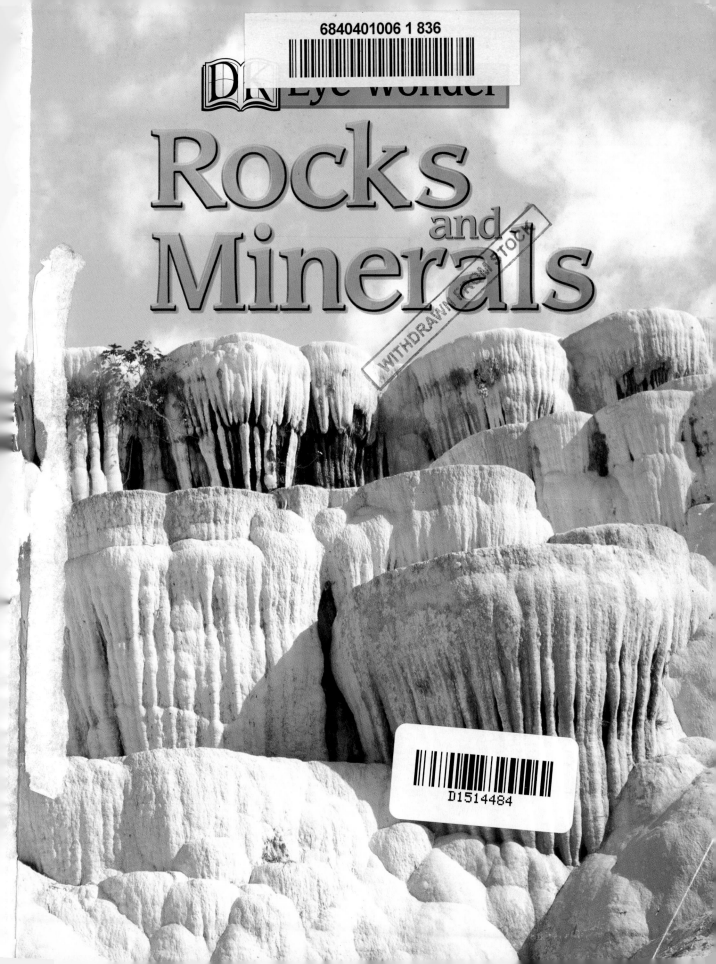

DK

LONDON, NEW YORK, MUNICH,
MELBOURNE, and DELHI

Written and edited by Caroline Bingham
Designed by Helen Chapman

Publishing manager Susan Leonard
Managing art editor Clare Shedden
Jacket design Chris Drew
Picture researcher Sarah Stewart-Richardson
Production Shivani Pandey
DTP Designer Almudena Díaz
Consultant Kim Dennis-Bryan PhD, FZS
With thanks to Victoria Long
for design assistance.

First published in hardback in Great Britain in 2004.
This paperback edition first published in 2007 by
Dorling Kindersley Limited
80 Strand, London WC2R 0RL

A CIP catalogue record for this book
is available from the British Library.

Hardback edition ISBN 978-1-4053-0090-2
Paperback edition ISBN 978-1-4053-2382-6

Colour reproduction by Colourscan, Singapore
Printed and bound in Italy by L.E.G.O.

Discover more at
www.dk.com

Contents

telephone

jewellery

car

clothes

Rocky Earth

Rocks and minerals are important. They make up much of our planet and are mined to provide many of the things around us, from cars to computers. Even your body contains minerals that keep you alive.

toothpaste

computer

you and me!

house

4

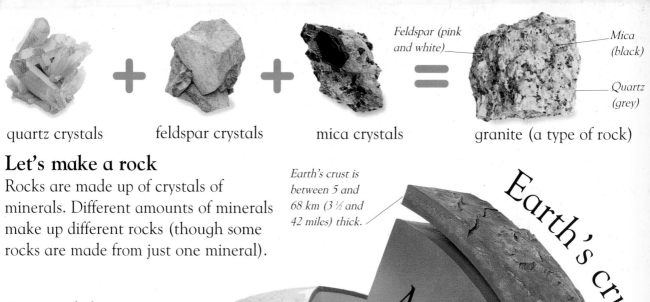

quartz crystals + feldspar crystals + mica crystals = granite (a type of rock)

Feldspar (pink and white)

Mica (black)

Quartz (grey)

Let's make a rock

Rocks are made up of crystals of minerals. Different amounts of minerals make up different rocks (though some rocks are made from just one mineral).

Earth's crust is between 5 and 68 km (3 ½ and 42 miles) thick.

Most of the crust and mantle is made from lots of different rocks, all squashed together.

Scientists believe the Earth was born about 4,600 million years ago.

Earth's crust

Mantle

Outer core

Core

Store cupboard

The things we use in our everyday lives come from our planet, Earth. The raw ingredients are all taken from the crust. We cannot drill any deeper.

Mineral facts

• Your body contains more than 60 minerals. Nine of these are essential for life.

• Some minerals take thousands of years to form. Some form in minutes.

Let's make shampoo

What forms the shampoo you use on your hair? Minerals, including those below!

coal tar + lithium clay + selenium = shampoo

A volcanic beginning

Squeeze clay in your hands and it oozes
between your fingers. This is a little like what
happens inside a volcano. The pressure grows
until the volcano erupts. Whoosh! It is the
first step in the formation of new rocks.

*When magma
leaves a volcano,
it is called lava.*

The magma is forced up inside the volcano.

*Previous eruptions
have formed a cone-
shaped exterior.*

*Magma (molten
rock) chamber.*

No place for a rock?
Deep, deep under the Earth's crust it is
hot enough to melt rock. This molten rock
sometimes builds up in chambers and bursts
through weak spots in the Earth's crust.

Avalanche of rock

A volcano erupts with such power that sometimes the eruption destroys a part of the volcano. Huge rocks shoot into the air.

Volcanic debris ranges from dust and ash to rocks the size of houses.

Just a cliff?

The eruption of a volcano can create deep layers of ash, dust, and rock at its base. It changes the landscape.

Shiprock Pinnacle is named after a ship as it looks a little like one.

Shiprock

Shiprock Pinnacle is all that remains of an ancient volcano. It is the hardened core.

Shiprock Pinnacle in New Mexico was once a plug of magma filling the chimney vent of a volcano.

Making of a rock

Do you think that all rocks look the same?
In fact, there are many different kinds of
rocks, but they can be divided into three
basic types, which are being formed (and
destroyed) as you read this book.

In the beginning

Earth's first rocks
were igneous rocks.
These form from
molten rock that has
cooled and hardened.

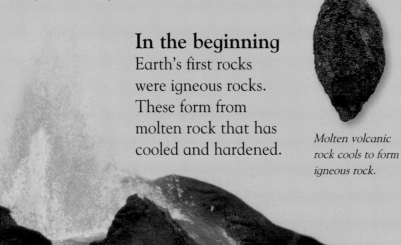

*Molten volcanic
rock cools to form
igneous rock.*

Chipping away

One way sedimentary rock
forms is when pieces of
rock are carried to the sea
where they create huge
piles of sediment. After
thousands of years these
cement together.

Sedimentary rock

Sediments are

Sediment settles on the bottom of seas, rivers, and lakes.

builds up in layers.

squashed together.

Getting hotter

Rub your hands together and they get hot. Metamorphic rock forms when rocks are squeezed and heated deep under the Earth's crust.

The pressure and heat as granite is forced up causes the development of the metamorphic rock marble.

Granite

Deep under the earth, rocks are being squashed and heated.

Marble

ROCKING AROUND

Over thousands of years, each type of rock can change into one of the others depending on what happens to it, from igneous to sedimentary to metamorphic.

Igneous rock

Igneous rocks form the greatest part of Earth's rocky crust, but can also be seen in the land around us. A famous igneous rock landscape is the Giant's Causeway in Northern Ireland.

Pele's hair looks like hair! It forms from sprays of lava.

Pumice stone is the only floating rock.

Pumice is an igneous rock from the heart of a volcano.

Obsidian has a shiny surface. It contains a lot of glass.

From hair to glass
A volcano produces a great variety of igneous rocks. Just take a look at the three examples shown above.

London's Tower Bridge uses granite.

Built to last
The most common igneous rock is granite. It is incredibly strong, and has been used for building for thousands of years.

Giant's Causeway

The Giant's Causeway in Antrim, Northern Ireland, formed when basalt lava cooled and shrank. This type of lava can create hexagonally shaped columns.

Legends say giants used the causeway as stepping stones.

Igneous facts

● "Igneous" comes from the Latin word for "fire".

● The more slowly that a rock cools from its molten form, the larger the crystals.

● Granite cools slowly and has large crystals. Obsidian, which cools quickly, has small crystals.

Sedimentary rock

Towering chalk cliffs are an amazing example of sedimentary rock. They are formed from the shells and skeletons of microscopic sea creatures. Just imagine how many are needed to build a cliff.

In places, these cliffs are 90 m (300 ft) high.

One by one
The sea creatures that break down to create chalk are tiny. It's thought that these cliffs grew by 0.5 mm (0.02 in) a year – that's about 180 of these creatures piled on top of one another.

Movements in the Earth's crust have lifted the cliffs out of the sea.

From plant to rock
Another way in which sedimentary rocks form is by the breakdown of plants. As they are buried, they are squeezed together, eventually forming coal.

Year 1...

From plant matter...

to peat...

12

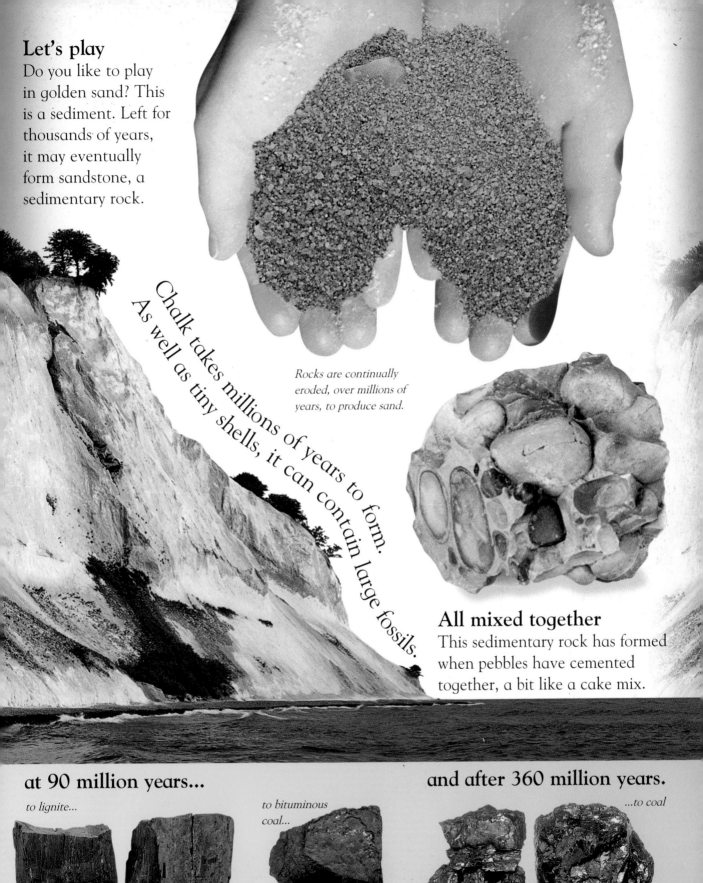

Let's play

Do you like to play in golden sand? This is a sediment. Left for thousands of years, it may eventually form sandstone, a sedimentary rock.

Rocks are continually eroded, over millions of years, to produce sand.

Chalk takes millions of years to form. As well as tiny shells, it can contain large fossils.

All mixed together

This sedimentary rock has formed when pebbles have cemented together, a bit like a cake mix.

at 90 million years...

to lignite...

to bituminous coal...

and after 360 million years.

...to coal

13

Metamorphic rock

"Metamorphic" comes from the ancient Greek words, *meta* (meaning change) and *morphe* (meaning form). When rocks are heated or compressed, this type of rock forms.

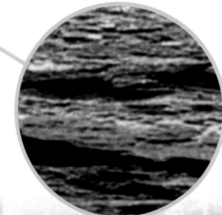

Underground changes
One way metamorphic rocks form is when mountains are pushed up out of the Earth's crust. Mountains and hills surround this old slate quarry.

A peek at slate
The metamorphic rock slate forms from mud and a rock called shale. The shale has been squeezed and compressed as mountains are pushed up. Slate splits easily into sheets.

Each block weighs thousands of tonnes.

Marble can be carved into statues.

Marble magic
Marble is a beautiful metamorphic rock. It is mined by being cut into huge blocks with strong cutting wires.

Icecream swirls

When rocks are heated, parts may begin to melt and run through a "host" rock. This makes swirly patterned metamorphic rock. The rock is called migmatite.

A shimmering palace

Polished marble looks stunning when used for building, and perhaps the world's most famous marble building is the Taj Mahal in India. The marble shimmers in the sun.

The dark host rock contains swirls of a lighter coloured rock.

Marble is formed from limestone.

Water cools the cutting equipment in a quarry.

Rocks from space

We cannot see it, but about 23 tonnes (25 tons) of dust rain down on Earth every day. This fine dust arrives from space. Occasionally a rock from space hits Earth; this is called a meteorite.

A meteorite hit

Meteorites are pieces of rock or metal that hit Earth. Some have broken off asteroids, large chunks of rock that orbit the Sun between Mars and Jupiter. Most are fragments of comets.

There is evidence that a massive meteorite hit Earth 65 million years ago, causing the dinosaurs to die out.

Meteorites hit Earth. Meteors burn up above it. Comets pass on by.

What's inside?

Meteorites from asteroids contain metals such as iron as well as rocks. Those from comets contain more rock than metal.

The pitted surface is created by the immense heat as the meteor "rubs" against the atmosphere.

ONCE IN A LIFETIME

One of the most famous comets, Halley's, was included in the Bayeux Tapestry, which was stitched more than 900 years ago. This comet passes Earth just once every 76 years. It last passed us in 1986.

Most meteors are the size of a small pebble.

A comet's tail is narrow but it can stretch for hundreds of kilometres

I spy a shooting star

Meteors or shooting stars can be seen as they burn up in Earth's atmosphere, usually more than 80 km (50 miles) above our heads.

Just passing

Comets are a bit like huge snowballs, but made of ice, gases, and dust. They orbit the Sun, developing long tails as they near Earth

What's that hole?

If a large meteorite hits Earth it can form a crater, changing the surroundings where it lands. It would take you about 30 minutes to walk across this meteorite crater in Australia.

This crater is so old that trees have grown in its base.

A large meteorite may be travelling at 40,000 km/h (25,000 mph) when it hits.

Hidden beauty

Brrrr! A cave is a damp, dark, chilly place. However, if you are lucky enough to visit a large cave that has been lit and opened to visitors, you'll discover incredibly beautiful shapes in the rocks.

This stream falls further than the length of a football pitch.

This cave has opened into a vast cavern.

Water damage

Over the course of thousands of years, a constant flow of water will eat away at a solid area of rock. After 100,000 years, this may have formed a small cave, which will continue to grow.

Build it up

Cave formations can be amazingly complicated. These slender shapes have built up gradually, as drops of water have deposited traces of a mineral called calcite.

A funny shape

Stalactites hang down while stalagmites grow up. It can take 1,000 years for these formations to grow less than a centimetre.

These volcanic caves were once mined for millstones.

Rock formations in caves build up drip by drip.

Soft centre

Have you ever eaten a hard sweet with a soft centre? Volcanic caves can form when soft lava pushes on through a hardened outer layer.

The tallest stalagmite in the world is the height of a six-storey house.

Breakdown

Rocks are not as permanent as you may think. From driving rain to frothy seas, when rocks are exposed to wind, water, glaciers, or shifts in temperature, changes begin to happen.

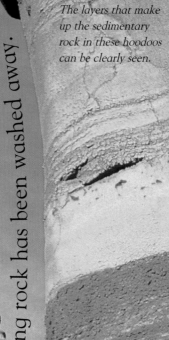

The layers that make up the sedimentary rock in these hoodoos can be clearly seen.

Attack by sea

A long time ago, these stacks were a part of Australia's coastline, but they have been cut off from the coast after an ongoing battering from the sea.

The surrounding rock has been washed away.

Attack by wind and water

Hoodoos are columns of soft sandstone topped by harder rock caps. The cap has protected the rock beneath it from being washed away by heavy downpours of rain.

Attack by acid rain

Pollution from cars and lorries attacks rock. The gases are carried in rainwater to make acids that eat into rock – as shown by the damage to this sculpture.

Attack by river

Over millions of years, the Colorado River has carved its way down into America's Grand Canyon, exposing rock faces 1,829 m (6,000 ft) deep.

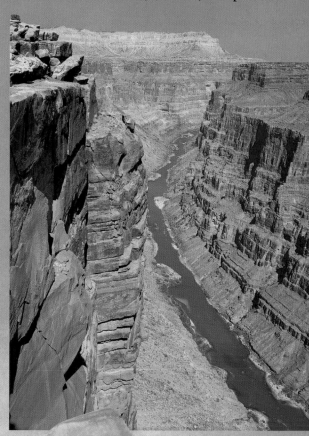

Hoodoos form spectacular shapes, all clustered together.

If a hoodoo loses its protective cap, the structure will soon begin to wear away.

Erosion causes sediment.

Erosion facts

● The wearing away of a landscape is known as erosion.

● Plants add to rock erosion as their roots burrow their way into cracks in rocks.

● When rocks are broken down where they stand, it is known as weathering.

The force of a glacier is enough to crumble rock.

Carving a path

A glacier is a huge mass of slow-moving ice. Born as snow builds up at the top of a mountain, it begins to force its way forward, picking up rocks and boulders as it moves.

Slow progress
Glaciers usually creep just a few centimetres a day. They end lower down the mountain where the water melts away, or at the coast where large blocks break off.

Adding the stripes

As a glacier works its way forward, it picks up all sorts of rocks and sediment. This forms darker streaks on the surface of the glacier.

A glacier carves a deep valley as it moves forwards.

From rock to flour!

The sides and base of a glacial valley are covered with plenty of scrapes and scratches. This scraping produces fine grains of rock, known as rock flour.

Rock flour is carried on down the glacier. Some is deposited in mountain lakes.

Sprinkle on the colour!

Mountain lakes are often incredible shades of turquoise blue. This is because of the rock flour fed into them by a melting glacier.

Tiny particles of rock in the water catch the light in a certain way.

Crystals

Have you ever cut a paper snowflake? Snowflakes are made from small ice crystals that collide and stick together. Crystals also form in rock, and can be cut and polished.

Beautiful colours

Many crystals come in a rich range of colours. This purple amethyst is a form of quartz. It can also be lilac or mauve.

From little to big

The tiny crystals that make up the endless golden sands of a desert are made of quartz. Quartz can also form gigantic crystals. The largest rock crystal was about 6 m (20 ft) long!

Crystals continue to grow as long as the surrounding conditions remain the same.

FANCY AN ICE LOLLY?

The word crystal comes from the Greek word *kyros*, which means "icy cold". The ancient Greeks thought quartz crystals were made of ice that had frozen so hard it could not melt.

24

Amethyst is prized for its colour.

Is it a thread?

Not all rock crystals are hard. This is a crystal called tremolite. It forms flexible strands similar to the fibres in material. But you wouldn't be able to sew with tremolite. It could make you ill.

Strands of tremolite have a silky, translucent look because light passes through the fibres.

Seems a bit salty

Salt may not seem like a rock, but it is a crystalline rock. In Bolivia there is even a hotel built from salt bricks, including the chairs and tables!

Salt crystals form when seawater evaporates.

The power to heal?

Some people believe that certain crystals have special powers. Jade is thought to help relaxation, lapis lazuli to help friendships.

Lapis lazuli

Polished jade

25

What a gem!

From sparkling diamonds to rich red rubies, some rocks are valuable and are known as gems. They are mined from the Earth at huge expense, cut and polished, and worked into jewellery.

Not just a rock

Most gemstones come from rocks. Just imagine that you were lucky enough to find this rock, with its red rubies.

A gem is a stone that has a beautiful colour.

Gemstones such as rubies can be rounded and polished or cut.

Shine on

A cut stone reflects more light, just like this diamond. A cut diamond may have as many as 58 flat sides. Diamond is the hardest mineral of all.

Which are you?

Do you know your birthstone? Some people believe it is lucky to wear a gem that is linked to their month of birth.

January	February	March	April	May
Garnet	*Amethyst*	*Aquamarine*	*Diamond*	*Emerald*

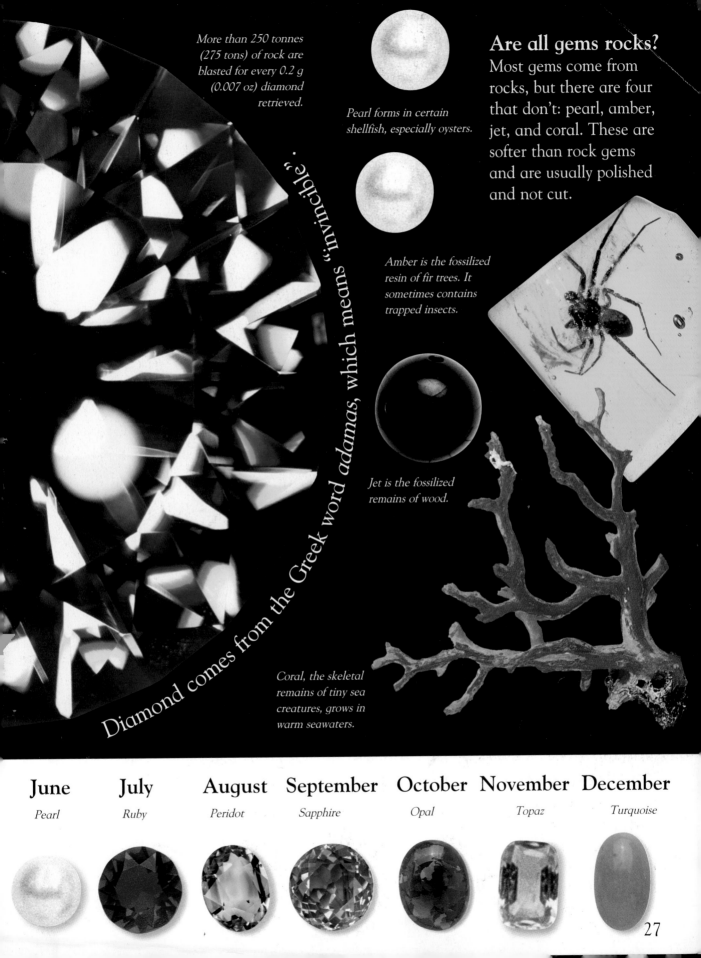

More than 250 tonnes (275 tons) of rock are blasted for every 0.2 g (0.007 oz) diamond retrieved.

Pearl forms in certain shellfish, especially oysters.

Are all gems rocks?

Most gems come from rocks, but there are four that don't: pearl, amber, jet, and coral. These are softer than rock gems and are usually polished and not cut.

Amber is the fossilized resin of fir trees. It sometimes contains trapped insects.

Diamond comes from the Greek word *adamas*, which means "invincible".

Jet is the fossilized remains of wood.

Coral, the skeletal remains of tiny sea creatures, grows in warm seawaters.

June	July	August	September	October	November	December
Pearl	Ruby	Peridot	Sapphire	Opal	Topaz	Turquoise

Precious metals

Gems are not the only treasures hidden deep within our rocky planet. Precious metals such as gold, silver, and platinum have long been mined and used to make objects of great beauty.

Gold is sometimes found in veins of quartz.

Gold

Bangkok in Thailand is home to the Golden Buddha, a religious statue made of solid gold. It weighs 5.5 tonnes (6 tons) – the weight of a small truck.

Platinum

Platinum is the most expensive metal of all. No wonder it was used to make this crown, part of the British Crown Jewels.

This rare platinum nugget weighs the same as 10 apples.

Silver is sometimes found with a delicate frond-like shape.

Silver

Seven hundred years ago silver was more valuable than gold. This soft metal was used for coins and jewellery – and for statues such as this Hindu figure.

29

Get that metal!

Some metals are held inside rocks as minerals – the rock that holds the mineral is known as the ore. Some ores are near the surface, some are deep underground.

Copper pipe

Some of the copper extracted from the mine below will be used to make copper pipes.

Boom!

An open-cast mine is a noisy place. The miners constantly blast away at the rock so they can take it away and extract the metal.

Let's make a hole

Most metals are collected from open-cast mines. This means that the surface is blasted and tonnes of rock are removed, truckload by truckload.

Mix them together...

Metals are often melted down and joined to other metals to make a stronger metal, an alloy.

An open-cast mine has a network of roads.

Copper ore　　*Tin ore*

...to get

When copper and tin are mixed together, they produce bronze, which can be used to make casts.

Bronze casts are made by pouring molten metal into a mould. It then sets.

A GIFT FROM SPACE

Not all metals come from the ground. Six thousand years ago, many people knew iron as "the metal from the sky", probably because the first iron people used came from meteorites.

31

Using rocks in art

Have you ever used a rock to draw? It's great fun to use chalk and scribble away on a pavement. The colours held inside some rocks and minerals have been used by artists for thousands of years.

Who needs paper?
Cave painters had no paper, so they used rock as their canvas. They used a mixture of materials to produce just four or five colours.

Cave paintings date back 20,000 years.

Cave painters used charcoal – the remains of burnt wood – to make black.

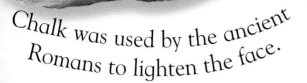

Chalk was used by the ancient Romans to lighten the face.

A light source

The sedimentary rock chalk is messy to use, but it is a fantastic material to use to show how light bounces off an object.

Gold was extracted from a mineral and used in this 600-year-old painting.

Cinnabar was first used in ancient China.

Rich reds

The powder of a mineral rock called cinnabar makes a brilliant red that was widely used in religious art in the Middle Ages.

Cinnabar is the main source of the poisonous metal mercury.

Rocks in history

A long time ago, somebody somewhere picked up a stone and used it as a tool. It was the beginning of something big as people found more and more ways in which to use rocks.

Just down the road
In the past there were no machines to fetch and carry, so people had to use what was available nearby. These roofs are covered with slate, taken from a local quarry.

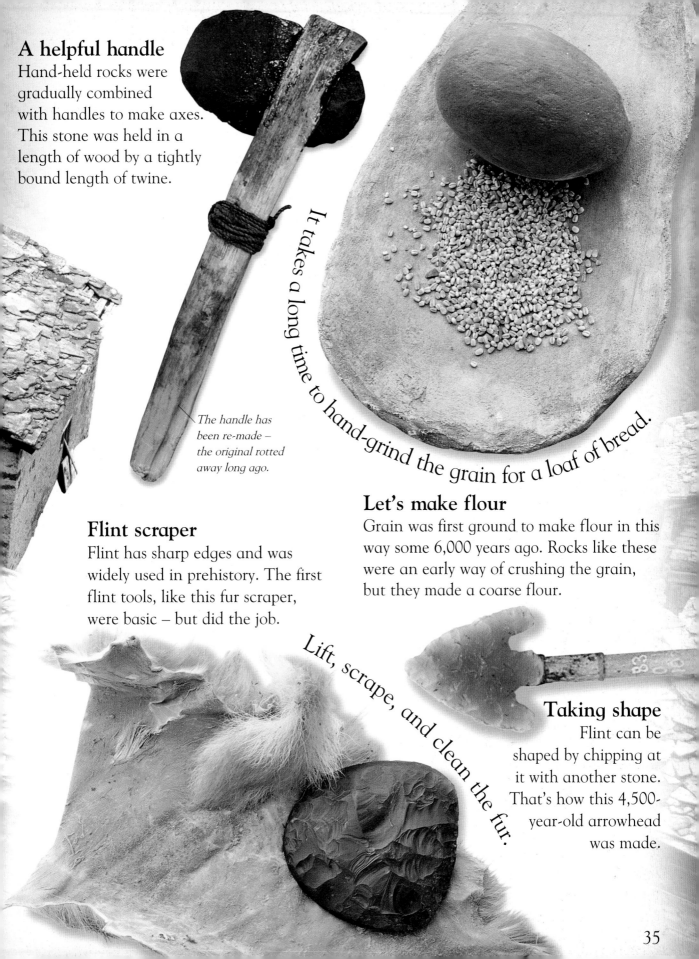

A helpful handle

Hand-held rocks were gradually combined with handles to make axes. This stone was held in a length of wood by a tightly bound length of twine.

The handle has been re-made – the original rotted away long ago.

It takes a long time to hand-grind the grain for a loaf of bread.

Let's make flour

Grain was first ground to make flour in this way some 6,000 years ago. Rocks like these were an early way of crushing the grain, but they made a coarse flour.

Flint scraper

Flint has sharp edges and was widely used in prehistory. The first flint tools, like this fur scraper, were basic – but did the job.

Lift, scrape, and clean the fur.

Taking shape

Flint can be shaped by chipping at it with another stone. That's how this 4,500-year-old arrowhead was made.

Building rocks

Take a look around you. Rocks are everywhere. In the pavement and the roads, in the houses in which we live, and in the skyscrapers that tower above us. They are the building blocks of modern cities.

From a mould
Bricks are made from clay, which is shaped in moulds and fired in huge ovens, called kilns, to bake it.

Skyscrapers
Skyscrapers are built from a variety of man-made materials on a steel framework. Many of these materials come from rocks that have been mined.

The building's steel framework is strong but also flexible in high winds.

sand + gravel + cement + water = concrete

Rock solid

Mix together the above ingredients and you will make concrete, a building material that quickly sets rock hard. It is used the world over.

The ancient Romans used concrete for their buildings.

Today, most window glass is coated to strengthen it.

Let in the light

Natural glass is as old as our planet – it is formed when lava cools. The first (small) man-made glass sheets were made about 1,000 years ago.

A touch of mystery

Some rocks and minerals look so
unusual that myths and legends
have grown up around them.
From Devil's toenails to
desert roses, the weird
and wonderful are
all around us.

*Wave Rock is
the height of a
three-storey house.*

A HISSING STONE?

Snakestones were once believed to be the
remains of coiled snakes turned to
stone by a 7th-century abbess
called St Hilda. They are
actually ammonites, the fossils
of shelled sea creatures, which
were sometimes given carved
snake heads.

Surf's up

Wave Rock in Australia is well named.
This massive rock is one and a half times
the length of a jumbo jet. It has formed
as much softer rock beneath the upper
lip has been worn away.

Taking root

Is it a tree root, or maybe an animal's burrow? No. This is fulgurite. It forms when lightning strikes sand and fuses the grains.

The forks follow the lightning's path.

Fulgurite is a glassy rock.

Are they toenail clippings?

These rocks were once believed to be the Devil's toenails. In fact, they are fossils – the remains of oyster shells.

Which way?

Magnetite is a magnetic mineral and was used in early compasses. We now use magnetite to produce iron – it contains a lot of iron.

Is it real?

Desert roses look very pretty, but they have no smell. They form in the desert from a mineral called barite.

The streaks are caused by minerals being washed down the rock by downpours of rain.

History in a rock

Rocks hide a lot of things, but perhaps the most exciting are the secrets rocks tell about life on Earth millions of years ago, when the dinosaurs ruled.

A special scientist called a paleontologist can discover how old a fossil is by

A dead beginning

A dinosaur lies down to die on a sandy shore. Perhaps it will not be eaten, and its skeleton will remain intact as its flesh rots away. The long path to becoming a fossil has begun.

What's that?

Imagine your footsteps being found by somebody in the future, preserved for ever in rock. Fossil footprints are a curious reminder of creatures long dead.

The fossils that have been discovered are only a tiny percentage of the animals that have lived.

Fossil dinosaur

The skeleton of this dinosaur has been preserved because the animal was covered in mud soon after death and squeezed between layers of sediment.

studying the rocks around it.

Big gnashers

Teeth are one of the most commonly found fossils – they last well because they are so hard. These belonged to a dinosaur called Iguanodon.

Clean up time

It takes a long time to extract a large fossil from the rock in which it is encased. The paleontologist working on it does not want to damage it.

The rock and dust surrounding a fossil are removed particle by particle if necessary.

This is the fossilized skeleton of a meat-eating dinosaur called Gasosaurus.

Fossil facts

- The parts of an animal most likely to fossilize are the hard bits: the bones, teeth, or shell.

- Fossils of footprints, or trackways, are called trace fossils.

- Fossils are found in sedimentary rock, such as limestone.

Hunting for rocks

Once you begin to learn about rocks and minerals, it's fun to go and look for some interesting rocks yourself. You may find a rock containing a fossil!

The spiral pattern of this long-fossilized ammonite can be seen in the Nautilus shells of today.

Leave no stone unturned
This child is looking for fossils. Depending on where in the world you live, you may have to be careful when looking for rocks: in some countries they hide dangerous creatures.

Start your rock collection by hunting for pebbles of different colours.

Mohs scale
Geologists use Mohs scale, which was set up in 1812, to measure a rock's hardness. The higher the number, the harder the rock.

1	2	3	4
Talc	Gypsum	Calcite	Fluorite

2.5
fingernail

42

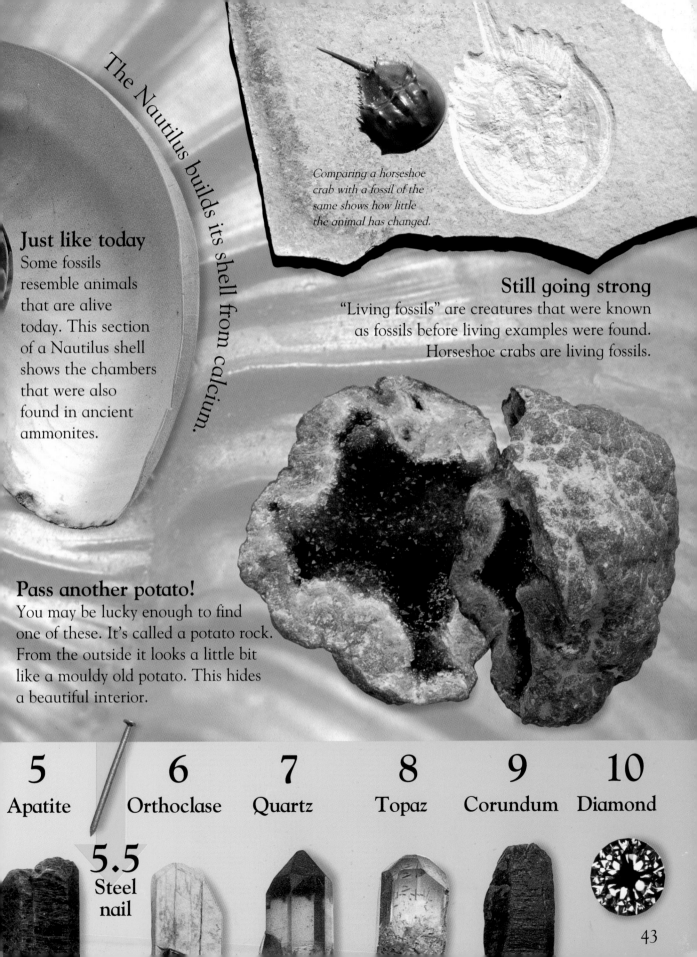

Comparing a horseshoe crab with a fossil of the same shows how little the animal has changed.

Just like today
Some fossils resemble animals that are alive today. This section of a Nautilus shell shows the chambers that were also found in ancient ammonites.

Still going strong
"Living fossils" are creatures that were known as fossils before living examples were found. Horseshoe crabs are living fossils.

Pass another potato!
You may be lucky enough to find one of these. It's called a potato rock. From the outside it looks a little bit like a mouldy old potato. This hides a beautiful interior.

5		6	7	8	9	10
Apatite	**5.5** Steel nail	**Orthoclase**	**Quartz**	**Topaz**	**Corundum**	**Diamond**

What does it make?

Rocks and minerals, and the metals that are taken from them, can be found in many of the everyday objects that surround you. Just take a look!

Clay is used in...

books

pencils

pottery

Fluorite is used in...

toothpaste

ceramics

water

Garnet is used in...

sandpaper

glass

jewellery

Limestone is used in...

cleaning products

books

concrete

Quartz is used in...

computers

radios

watch batteries

Silica sand is used in...

televisions

glass

plastic buckets

Silver is used in...

telephones

cameras

picture frames

Sulphur is used in...

films

matches

paper

Talc is used in...

paint

ceramics

talcum powder

Glossary

Here are the meanings of some words it is useful to know
when learning about rocks and minerals.

Alloy a metal that is made from combining two or more metals.

Basalt one of the most common forms of igneous rock.

Coal a rock made from plants that have been buried and squeezed over millions of years.

Crystal a naturally occurring substance with a specific make up which forms particular types of mineral.

Erosion the wearing away of a landscape.

Fossil the preserved remains of ancient life or evidence of their activity.

Glacier a mass of ice or snow which flows under its own weight.

Igneous rock rock made from molten rock that has cooled and hardened.